FHA Loan Limits, Down Payment & Closing Costs

How Much You Can Borrow and How to Bring Less Money to the Closing Table

By Joseph G. Correa

Licensed Mortgage Broker, Finibi Mortgage

Copyright & Legal Notice

Published by Live Stronger Faster

First Edition, 2026

Table of Contents

Foreword

For many aspiring homeowners, the biggest obstacle to buying a home is not desire, discipline, or even income—it is uncertainty. Uncertainty about how much home they can actually afford. Uncertainty about how much money they truly need to bring to the closing table. Uncertainty about what lenders will allow, what programs will approve them, and whether the numbers they see online apply to their real situation. FHA loans were created to reduce these barriers, yet over time they have become surrounded by confusion, outdated assumptions, and half-truths that leave borrowers discouraged before they ever begin. This book exists to replace uncertainty with clarity and to transform vague assumptions into precise, actionable knowledge. Understanding FHA loan limits, down payments, and closing costs is not just a technical exercise—it is the foundation upon which confident homeownership and long-term wealth are built.

One of the most damaging myths in real estate is the idea that homeownership requires a large amount of cash upfront. For decades, potential buyers have delayed or abandoned their plans because they believed they needed twenty percent down, perfect credit, or tens of thousands of dollars in savings. FHA loans were specifically designed to challenge this narrative.

They were built to open doors for working families, first-time buyers, self-employed individuals, and borrowers who may not fit traditional lending molds. Yet without a clear understanding of how FHA loan limits work, how minimum down payments are calculated, and how closing costs can be reduced or covered, borrowers often underestimate what is possible. This book brings those possibilities into focus by explaining not only the rules, but how they are applied in real-world transactions across different markets and borrower profiles.

Loan limits are often misunderstood as fixed ceilings that restrict opportunity, when in reality they are flexible benchmarks that vary by location, household structure, and property type. Many borrowers assume they cannot buy in certain areas because they believe FHA loan limits are too low, only to discover later that the limits in their county are higher than expected, or that multi-unit properties allow for significantly increased borrowing power. Others assume loan limits automatically dictate their purchasing power without understanding how income, debt ratios, and compensating factors interact with those limits. This book reframes loan limits not as restrictions, but as tools—tools that, when understood correctly, can be used strategically to maximize purchasing power while staying within safe and sustainable lending guidelines. Down payments are another area where misunderstanding creates unnecessary fear. While FHA loans are known for their low minimum down payment requirements, many borrowers do not understand how those requirements are determined, how credit scores influence down payment percentages, or how gift funds, assistance programs, and seller contributions can dramatically reduce out-of-pocket costs. Some buyers believe that a low down payment automatically leads to higher risk or poorer loan terms, while others incorrectly assume that saving more money always leads to better outcomes. The reality is far more nuanced. This book explains how FHA down payments work in practice, how to prepare for them intelligently, and how to align cash resources with long-term financial goals rather than arbitrary savings targets.

Closing costs are often the most intimidating and least transparent part of the homebuying process. Borrowers frequently encounter numbers at the end of a transaction that feel unexpected or overwhelming, even when the purchase price and interest rate are well understood. This confusion is rarely the borrower's fault. Closing costs vary by state, lender, transaction structure, and even time of year, and they are often explained poorly or too late in the process. FHA loans provide unique opportunities to manage, reduce, and sometimes eliminate many of these costs through seller credits, lender credits, and program-specific allowances. This book demystifies closing costs by breaking them down into understandable components and showing how informed borrowers can approach them proactively instead of reactively.

Beyond the mechanics, this book is about mindset. Borrowers who understand loan limits, down payments, and closing costs approach homeownership differently. They negotiate with confidence instead of fear. They evaluate properties strategically instead of emotionally. They plan their finances with intention instead of guesswork. Knowledge changes the borrower from a passive participant into an active decision-maker. FHA loans are not merely financing tools; they are leverage instruments that, when used correctly, allow borrowers to preserve cash, protect liquidity, and create pathways to future investments and refinances. This book lays the groundwork for that strategic thinking by teaching borrowers how to see the numbers behind the loan as part of a broader wealth-building plan.

It is also important to recognize that FHA guidelines were not designed to trap borrowers in risky situations, but to balance accessibility with sustainability. Loan limits exist to prevent overextension. Down payment requirements are structured to ensure commitment without exclusion. Closing cost rules are designed to protect both borrowers and lenders from hidden risks. When these elements are understood as protective mechanisms rather than obstacles, borrowers can work within them to achieve outcomes that are both attainable and responsible. This book emphasizes that FHA success is not about stretching to the maximum allowable number, but about choosing the right structure for long-term stability and growth.

As part of *The FHA Homeownership & Wealth Series*, this book builds upon the foundation laid in the earlier volumes while preparing the reader for more advanced strategies discussed later in the series. Understanding how much you can borrow and how much cash you truly need is essential before exploring refinancing, cash-out strategies, or multi-unit investing. This book serves as a bridge between entry-level understanding and advanced application. It equips readers with the numerical literacy needed to move forward confidently, whether they are buying their first home, upgrading to a larger property, or planning future wealth moves through FHA-backed financing.

The goal of this foreword is not merely to introduce the topic, but to reframe the reader's relationship with money, lending, and opportunity. FHA loan limits, down payments, and closing costs are not barriers meant to keep borrowers out—they are structures designed to bring borrowers in safely. When understood clearly, they become predictable, manageable, and even empowering. This book invites readers to replace fear with facts, assumptions with clarity, and hesitation with informed action. By the time the final page is turned, the reader will not only understand the numbers behind FHA loans, but will also understand how to use them as stepping stones toward lasting homeownership and financial growth.

Ultimately, this book exists because homeownership should not feel like a mystery reserved for insiders. It should be a transparent, navigable process that rewards preparation, education, and intention. FHA loans were created to serve that purpose, and this book is written to ensure they do. As you begin this chapter of the series, you are not just learning about loan limits, down payments, and closing costs—you are learning how to take control of your buying power, protect your cash, and position yourself for a future where homeownership is not just a milestone, but a foundation for wealth.

Chapter 1

The Real Cost of Buying a Home — What FHA Borrowers Need to Understand First

Before any borrower can make confident decisions about FHA loan limits, down payments, or closing costs, they must first understand a simple but often misunderstood truth: the price of a home is not the same as the cost of buying a home. Many buyers fixate on the listing price alone, believing that if they can afford the monthly payment shown in an online calculator, they are ready to move forward. In reality, the purchase price is only one piece of a larger financial equation. FHA loans are designed to make homeownership more accessible, but accessibility does not mean guesswork. It means understanding how the numbers work together so that borrowers can plan, budget, and negotiate from a position of clarity rather than fear.

One of the most common mistakes FHA borrowers make is assuming that affordability is determined by income alone. While income plays an important role, lenders evaluate affordability using a combination of loan limits, debt-to-income ratios, down payment requirements, mortgage insurance, interest rates, and closing costs. These elements are interconnected. A change in one affects the others. FHA guidelines allow flexibility, but flexibility does not eliminate structure. This chapter establishes the framework for understanding that structure so borrowers can see how much they can realistically buy, how much cash they need, and how to avoid surprises late in the process.

FHA loan limits are often misunderstood as arbitrary numbers imposed by the government, when in fact they are carefully calculated thresholds based on median home prices in specific geographic areas. These limits are updated annually and vary by county, meaning a borrower's purchasing power can change significantly depending on where they plan to buy. A borrower shopping in one county may qualify for a much higher FHA loan amount than a borrower with the same income shopping just a few miles away. Understanding this geographic component early allows borrowers to make smarter decisions about location, property type, and long-term affordability.

Equally important is understanding that loan limits do not automatically determine how much a borrower will be approved for. The maximum loan amount allowed by FHA is only relevant if the borrower's income, debts, and credit profile support that amount. Many borrowers mistakenly believe that because FHA allows a certain loan size, they should aim for that maximum. In reality, the smartest borrowers evaluate their comfort level, future plans, and cash reserves before deciding how much to borrow. FHA loans are powerful tools, but like any tool, they must be used intentionally.

Down payments are another area where perception often differs from reality. FHA is widely known for allowing low down payments, sometimes as low as 3.5 percent. However, borrowers frequently misunderstand how that percentage is calculated, what factors influence it, and how it interacts with closing costs. A low down payment does not mean a borrower can walk into a closing with almost no funds, nor does it mean they are financially unprepared. FHA loans allow borrowers to preserve cash, which can be strategically advantageous when done correctly. This chapter introduces the concept that cash preservation is not weakness; it is often a smart financial move.

Closing costs are typically the least understood part of the homebuying process. Many borrowers hear the term without fully grasping what it includes. Closing costs are not a single fee but a collection of expenses related to originating the loan, transferring ownership, recording documents, and establishing escrow accounts. FHA loans place limits on certain fees and allow seller contributions to cover many of these costs, but borrowers must still understand how they are calculated and disclosed. Without this understanding, buyers may feel blindsided when they receive their initial loan estimate or closing disclosure.

This chapter emphasizes that FHA borrowers are not expected to memorize formulas or become mortgage professionals. However, they are expected to understand the logic behind the numbers that determine their purchase. When borrowers understand how loan limits, down payments, and closing costs fit together, they gain the ability to ask better questions, recognize red flags, and avoid costly mistakes. Knowledge shifts the borrower's role from passive applicant to informed participant.

Another critical concept introduced in this chapter is the difference between approval and affordability. Just because a lender approves a borrower for a certain amount does not mean that amount aligns with the borrower's lifestyle, savings goals, or long-term financial health. FHA guidelines are designed to allow access, not to dictate personal financial choices. This chapter encourages borrowers to think beyond the minimum requirements and consider how their mortgage fits into their broader financial picture, including emergency savings, retirement planning, and future housing goals.

Finally, this chapter sets the tone for the rest of the book by reinforcing that FHA loans are not "lesser" loans or temporary solutions. They are legitimate, powerful financing tools used by millions of homeowners across income levels and professions. When borrowers understand the real cost of buying a home and how FHA structures that cost, they are better positioned to use FHA loans not just to buy a house, but to build stability and long-term wealth. With this foundation in place, the chapters that follow will break down each component in greater detail, turning complexity into clarity and uncertainty into confidence.

"Maria's Numbers Don't Lie"

Maria had always believed that buying a home was something she would do "someday," a vague future goal that felt just out of reach. She earned $62,000 a year, had a steady job, and paid her bills on time, but the idea of needing a massive down payment kept her renting year after year. One afternoon, she finally decided to sit down and look at the numbers instead of the assumptions. She pulled out a notebook, a calculator, and wrote one simple question at the top of the page: What does buying a home with FHA actually cost?

Maria started with the purchase price. Homes in her area averaged around $300,000. She assumed that meant she needed $60,000 for a down payment because she had always heard about twenty percent. Then she learned FHA required only 3.5 percent. She did the math. Three and a half percent of $300,000 was $10,500. That single calculation immediately changed how the goal felt. Ten thousand five hundred dollars was still significant, but it was no longer impossible. It was something she could plan for.

Next, Maria looked at loan limits in her county and discovered the FHA limit was $498,257. That meant her $300,000 target home was well within FHA guidelines. She realized that the loan limit was not the obstacle she imagined. It simply defined the maximum, not her obligation. She wrote down another number. If she put $10,500 down, her base loan amount would be $289,500. The math was straightforward, and seeing it on paper made it real.

Then came closing costs. Maria estimated closing costs at about 3 percent of the purchase price, which came out to $9,000. At first, that number made her nervous again. But instead of panicking, she kept going. She learned that FHA allows sellers to contribute up to 6 percent of the purchase price toward closing costs. Six percent of $300,000 was $18,000. That meant the seller could potentially cover all $9,000 in closing costs and still be within FHA rules. Maria wrote "possible seller credit" next to the number and underlined it.

Finally, Maria added up her true out-of-pocket cost. If the seller covered closing costs, she would need $10,500 for the down payment plus maybe a few thousand for reserves and inspections. Suddenly, the total cash needed was closer to $13,000 to $15,000, not the $70,000 she had imagined for years. The math didn't lie. The fear had come from misinformation, not reality.

By the time Maria closed her notebook, she wasn't just excited. She was calm. The numbers made sense. She realized that FHA wasn't a shortcut or a compromise. It was a structured system designed to make ownership achievable. For the first time, buying a home wasn't a dream based on hope. It was a plan based on math.

Chapter 2

FHA Loan Limits Decoded — How Location, Property Type, and Strategy Shape Your Buying Power

One of the most misunderstood aspects of FHA financing is the concept of loan limits. Many borrowers hear the phrase and immediately assume restriction, limitation, or disqualification. In reality, FHA loan limits are not designed to prevent borrowers from buying homes; they are designed to align borrowing power with local housing markets while maintaining long-term loan stability. Understanding how these limits work is essential because they define the maximum framework within which all other FHA calculations—down payment, mortgage insurance, and affordability—are built. Without this understanding, borrowers often underestimate their options or pursue properties that do not align with FHA guidelines, leading to frustration and lost opportunities.

FHA loan limits are set annually and vary by county, reflecting differences in median home prices across the country. This means that two borrowers with identical incomes, credit profiles, and financial histories can have very different FHA loan ceilings simply because they are buying in different locations. High-cost areas are assigned higher FHA limits, while lower-cost areas have lower limits. This geographic adjustment is intentional. FHA is designed to provide access across diverse markets, not to apply a one-size-fits-all cap that ignores local reality. Borrowers who understand this early can make more strategic decisions about where they shop and what types of properties they consider.

Another critical point often overlooked is that FHA loan limits apply to the loan amount, not the purchase price. This distinction matters because the down payment reduces the loan amount. A borrower purchasing a home slightly above the FHA loan limit may still qualify if the required down payment brings the loan amount within allowable limits. Conversely, a borrower purchasing well below the limit may still be constrained by income or debt ratios. Loan limits set the ceiling, but borrower qualification determines how close one can realistically get to that ceiling.

Property type also plays a major role in FHA loan limits. FHA allows borrowers to purchase not only single-family homes, but also multi-unit properties with up to four units, as long as the borrower occupies one of them as a primary residence. Each additional unit increases the allowable FHA loan limit. This means a borrower purchasing a duplex, triplex, or fourplex can qualify for a significantly higher loan amount than a borrower purchasing a single-family home in the same county. For buyers interested in combining homeownership with rental income, understanding these limits can unlock opportunities that would otherwise remain invisible.

However, higher loan limits do not automatically mean higher approval amounts. FHA still evaluates borrower income, existing debts, and overall risk profile. Many borrowers mistakenly believe that because FHA allows a higher limit for a multi-unit property, they will automatically qualify for it. In reality, lenders must still determine whether the borrower can support the payment. While projected rental income from additional units can help offset the mortgage payment, it does not eliminate the need for sufficient personal income and acceptable debt ratios. This chapter emphasizes that loan limits expand opportunity, but they do not replace underwriting fundamentals.

Another misconception is that FHA loan limits dictate what borrowers should spend. In truth, the limit simply defines what is permitted, not what is optimal. Smart borrowers use loan limits as reference points, not targets. They consider future income stability, lifestyle costs, emergency reserves, and long-term plans before deciding how much home to buy. FHA loans are designed to support sustainable homeownership, not financial strain. Borrowers who approach loan limits strategically often find themselves better positioned for future refinancing or wealth-building moves.

This chapter also introduces the idea that loan limits can be leveraged as part of a broader strategy. For example, a borrower may choose a property type or location specifically because it aligns better with FHA limits and long-term goals. A buyer priced out of a single-family home in one county may discover that a neighboring county offers higher limits relative to home prices. Others may intentionally choose a multi-unit property to maximize borrowing power while generating rental income. These are not loopholes; they are features of the FHA system designed to accommodate diverse borrower needs.

Finally, understanding FHA loan limits reduces anxiety during the home search. Borrowers who know their county limit, understand how it applies to different property types, and recognize how down payments interact with loan amounts approach the process with clarity. They are less likely to waste time on properties that cannot be financed and more likely to negotiate confidently within FHA guidelines. This chapter lays the groundwork for informed decision-making by transforming loan limits from a vague concept into a practical tool that borrowers can use to shape their homeownership journey intentionally and intelligently.

"David's Map Wasn't the Problem"

David had been searching for a home for six months and couldn't understand why nothing ever worked. Every time he found a property he liked, someone told him it was "too expensive for FHA." The phrase echoed in his head until it became a belief. He earned $74,000 a year, had solid credit, and saved $18,000, yet he felt stuck. One evening, instead of scrolling listings, David decided to look at numbers.

He started by checking the FHA loan limit in his county. The limit for a single-family home was $472,030. The homes he liked were listed around $485,000. At first glance, that seemed like a dead end. Then David remembered something important: FHA limits applied to the loan amount, not the purchase price. He wrote down the numbers. If he bought a $485,000 home and put 3.5 percent down, that would be $16,975. Subtracting that from the purchase price gave him a base loan amount of $468,025. That number was below the FHA limit. The home was never "too expensive." The math simply hadn't been done.

Encouraged, David went further. He noticed that duplexes in his area were priced slightly higher, around $520,000. The FHA loan limit for a duplex in his county was $604,400. Again, he did the math. A 3.5 percent down payment on $520,000 was $18,200. The resulting loan amount was

$501,800, well under the duplex limit. On top of that, projected rental income from the second unit could offset part of the mortgage payment. The numbers didn't just work; they worked better than expected.

David compared scenarios. Single-family home at $485,000 meant one payment supported entirely by his income. Duplex at $520,000 meant part of the payment supported by rent. Even though the duplex cost more, the math showed a lower effective monthly burden. What had once felt like a limitation turned out to be an opportunity hidden behind misunderstood rules.

By the end of the night, David realized the problem had never been FHA or his finances. The problem was that he had been shopping without understanding the map. Once he learned how loan limits really worked, the path forward became obvious. FHA wasn't limiting his options. It was quietly offering more than he ever realized.

Chapter 3

The Power of the FHA Down Payment – Why Less Cash Can Mean More Control

Few topics in homeownership generate as much confusion and emotional weight as the down payment. For many borrowers, the down payment represents a psychological barrier rather than a financial one, shaped by decades of advice suggesting that bigger is always better and that less cash down equals higher risk. FHA loans challenge this belief by design. They allow borrowers to enter homeownership with a low down payment not because standards are weaker, but because the program recognizes that access, liquidity, and long-term stability often matter more than upfront cash. Understanding how FHA down payments work is essential for borrowers who want to make informed decisions rather than defaulting to outdated assumptions.

The FHA minimum down payment of 3.5 percent is one of the program's most powerful features, yet it is also one of the most misunderstood. This percentage is calculated based on the purchase price, not the loan amount, and it applies to borrowers who meet FHA's minimum credit requirements. Many buyers incorrectly believe that a low down payment automatically results in higher monthly payments that make ownership unsustainable. In reality, the difference between a 3.5 percent down payment and a larger down payment is often far smaller than expected, especially when compared to the benefits of retaining cash reserves.

One of the most important concepts for FHA borrowers to understand is liquidity. Cash in the bank provides flexibility, protection, and options. When borrowers use all of their savings to increase their down payment, they may feel more secure psychologically, but they often leave themselves financially exposed. FHA's low down payment structure allows borrowers to preserve cash for emergencies, repairs, furnishings, or future opportunities. This liquidity can be the difference between long-term success and short-term stress, particularly for first-time buyers or households with variable income.

Credit score plays a role in determining FHA down payment requirements, but not in the way many borrowers assume. FHA allows the minimum 3.5 percent down payment for borrowers who meet the program's credit thresholds, and higher down payments are not automatically required simply because a borrower has average or imperfect credit. This is a critical distinction. FHA is designed to evaluate overall risk, not to penalize borrowers unnecessarily. Understanding this allows borrowers to plan realistically instead of over-saving out of fear. Another powerful feature of FHA down payments is flexibility in sourcing funds. FHA permits down payments to come from personal savings, gift funds from eligible donors, and certain assistance programs. This flexibility acknowledges that not all borrowers build wealth in the same way. For many families, pooled resources or assistance from relatives represent responsible financial planning, not weakness. FHA's acceptance of these sources allows borrowers to enter homeownership sooner while still maintaining compliance and transparency.

It is also important to understand that a lower down payment does not mean a borrower lacks commitment. FHA borrowers still undergo full underwriting, income verification, and risk assessment. The difference lies in structure, not standards. FHA spreads risk across mortgage insurance and program safeguards so that borrowers are not forced to choose between homeownership and financial security. This chapter reinforces that FHA's low down payment is a strategic design choice, not a shortcut.

Borrowers must also consider opportunity cost. Every dollar placed into a down payment is a dollar no longer available for other purposes. While paying more upfront can reduce loan balance slightly, it may delay other financial goals such as building emergency savings, investing, or preparing for future moves. FHA borrowers who understand opportunity cost are better equipped to decide how much cash to deploy and how much to retain. The smartest down payment is not always the largest one, but the one that aligns with the borrower's broader financial strategy.

This chapter encourages borrowers to shift their mindset from minimizing loan size at all costs to optimizing overall financial health. FHA down payments are a tool, not a test. They allow borrowers to enter ownership with balance rather than depletion. When used intentionally, they can provide stability today while preserving flexibility for tomorrow. With this understanding, borrowers can approach the next stages of the FHA process with confidence, knowing that their down payment choice supports both ownership and long-term wealth.

"Carlos Chose the Smaller Number"

Carlos had saved $45,000 over eight years and was proud of it. When he decided to buy a home, his instinct was to use as much of that money as possible for the down payment. He believed that putting more down was the responsible thing to do. The home he wanted was priced at $360,000, and he immediately calculated a twenty percent down payment. That number came out to $72,000, which meant he would need to drain his savings and still come up short. The realization almost stopped him from moving forward. Instead of giving up, Carlos decided to explore FHA. He learned that the minimum down payment was 3.5 percent. He calculated it carefully. Three and a half percent of $360,000 was $12,600. That number surprised him. It felt almost too low to be responsible. But Carlos kept going. With a $12,600 down payment, his base loan amount would be $347,400. He compared that to a hypothetical scenario where he put $40,000 down instead. In that case, the loan amount would be $320,000. The difference in loan balance was $27,400.

Carlos then compared monthly payments. At a fixed interest rate, the payment difference between the two loan amounts was less than $150 per month. That number gave him pause. He realized he was considering tying up an extra $27,400 upfront to save $150 per month. When he multiplied $150 by twelve months, the annual savings was $1,800. It would take more than fifteen years to recover the extra cash he put down, not accounting for inflation or opportunity cost.

Carlos looked at his savings again. If he used only $12,600 for the down payment, he would still have over $30,000 in reserves. That money could cover emergencies, home repairs, or even future investments. He realized that the smaller down payment didn't make him less prepared. It made him more flexible. When Carlos closed on his home, he felt something he hadn't expected. Instead of anxiety about his mortgage balance, he felt control. The math showed him that the smartest choice wasn't the biggest number on paper. It was the number that kept his financial life balanced. FHA didn't lower his standards. It gave him options.

Chapter 4

How Smart FHA Buyers Bring Less Cash to Closing Without Cutting Corners

One of the most powerful advantages of FHA financing is not simply the low down payment or flexible credit standards, but the ability to structure a transaction in a way that minimizes out-of-pocket cash while remaining fully compliant with lending rules. Many borrowers believe that the amount of money they must bring to closing is fixed once they choose a home price and loan program. In reality, the cash required at closing is one of the most flexible elements of an FHA transaction. Borrowers who understand how FHA rules interact with negotiation, pricing, and credits can often reduce their upfront cash requirement dramatically without increasing financial risk.

The first misconception that must be addressed is the idea that bringing less cash to closing means taking on a worse deal. This belief is rooted in traditional lending culture, where large down payments and high upfront costs were equated with strength and responsibility. FHA financing operates under a different philosophy. It prioritizes sustainable homeownership over cash depletion. Bringing less cash to closing does not weaken the borrower's position; in many cases, it strengthens it by preserving liquidity, reducing financial stress, and allowing room for future expenses such as maintenance, repairs, or emergency savings.

A key strategy FHA borrowers must understand is the relationship between purchase price and seller concessions. FHA allows sellers to contribute up to six percent of the purchase price toward the buyer's closing costs and prepaid expenses. This rule alone can shift the entire financial structure of a transaction. Instead of viewing the list price as a rigid number, savvy borrowers view it as a starting point for structuring terms. In some cases, a slightly higher purchase price combined with seller-paid closing costs can result in a significantly lower cash requirement for the buyer, even if the loan amount increases modestly.

This strategy works because mortgage financing spreads cost over time, while cash at closing is an immediate drain. When a borrower increases the purchase price by a small amount to receive a larger seller credit, the impact on the monthly payment is often minimal compared to the benefit of preserving thousands of dollars in cash. FHA borrowers who understand this tradeoff can make decisions based on long-term stability rather than short-term fear of loan balances. Another overlooked factor is how appraisal value interacts with negotiated pricing. FHA requires the home to appraise at or above the purchase price. When a property supports the value, seller concessions do not weaken the transaction. They simply reallocate where the money flows. Borrowers who work with knowledgeable agents and lenders can structure offers that remain competitive while protecting their cash position. This chapter emphasizes that FHA buyers are not asking for special treatment; they are using built-in program features as intended.

Lender credits also provide another layer of flexibility. By accepting a slightly higher interest rate, borrowers can receive lender credits that offset closing costs. This option is particularly useful for buyers who expect to refinance in the future or who prioritize liquidity over long-term interest savings. FHA borrowers must understand that interest rate decisions are not purely emotional or binary. They are strategic tools. When used thoughtfully, lender credits can eliminate thousands of dollars in upfront costs with only a modest increase in monthly payment.

Timing also plays a role in reducing cash to close. Closing near the end of the month reduces prepaid interest. Understanding escrow timing can prevent overfunding accounts unnecessarily. Even choosing when to lock a rate can influence credits and pricing. None of these strategies require bending rules or taking on excessive risk. They simply require awareness and planning. This chapter also challenges the idea that borrowers should exhaust savings to "feel safe." Financial safety does not come from emptying accounts; it comes from maintaining buffers. FHA's structure allows borrowers to keep reserves while still meeting ownership requirements. This is especially important for first-time buyers who may face unexpected expenses in the first year of ownership. Homes are living assets, not static investments. Liquidity matters.

Ultimately, this chapter reframes the closing table as a place of strategy rather than sacrifice. FHA borrowers who understand how to structure offers, negotiate credits, and balance loan terms walk away from closing not exhausted, but empowered. Bringing less cash to closing is not about doing less. It is about doing it smarter. FHA provides the framework. The borrower provides the intention.

"Marcus Didn't Pay Twice"

Marcus found a home listed at $340,000 and immediately started calculating how much money he would need. Using FHA's 3.5 percent down payment, he calculated $11,900. He estimated closing costs at roughly $10,000. His initial assumption was that he would need nearly $22,000 to close. That number bothered him because it would leave him with very little savings afterward. Instead of backing out, Marcus decided to run scenarios. He noticed that FHA allowed seller contributions up to six percent. Six percent of $340,000 was $20,400. His estimated closing costs were well below that number. Marcus and his agent decided to structure the offer differently. Instead of offering $340,000 with no credits, they offered $350,000 with $10,000 in seller-paid closing costs.

Marcus recalculated. His new down payment at 3.5 percent of $350,000 was $12,250. His loan amount increased by $10,000, but his cash requirement dropped sharply. Instead of needing $22,000, he now needed closer to $12,500 plus minor prepaid adjustments. That meant he preserved nearly $9,500 in savings.

Marcus looked at the monthly payment difference. Financing an extra $10,000 increased his payment by less than $60 per month. When he multiplied that $60 by twelve, the annual difference was $720. He compared that to the $9,500 he preserved at closing. It would take over thirteen years for the increased payment to equal the cash he kept.

On closing day, Marcus still had over $18,000 in the bank after buying his home. When the water heater failed six months later, he didn't panic. The math he did before closing protected him after closing. FHA didn't cost him more. It helped him avoid paying twice—once at the table and again in stress.

Chapter 5

From Approval to Comfort – Why the Maximum Loan Is Rarely the Best Loan

One of the most subtle traps FHA borrowers fall into is confusing what they are approved for with what they should actually borrow. When a lender issues a preapproval, it often reflects the maximum loan amount allowed under FHA guidelines based on income, credit, and debt ratios. While this number can feel empowering, it can also quietly steer borrowers toward decisions that create unnecessary financial strain. FHA loans are designed to provide access, not pressure. Understanding the difference between approval and comfort is essential for borrowers who want ownership to enhance their lives rather than dominate them.

FHA underwriting uses debt-to-income ratios to evaluate affordability, and these ratios allow for more flexibility than many conventional loan programs. This flexibility helps borrowers qualify, but it does not mean every borrower should aim for the highest possible number. Debt ratios measure capacity, not quality of life. A borrower can technically afford a payment on paper while still feeling constrained in real life by rising expenses, lifestyle needs, or future goals. This chapter challenges borrowers to look beyond the approval letter and consider how the mortgage fits into their broader financial picture.

Another important factor often overlooked is how monthly housing costs extend beyond the principal and interest payment. FHA borrowers must account for mortgage insurance premiums, property taxes, homeowners insurance, and in some cases homeowners association dues. When these costs are added together, the difference between a comfortable payment and a stressful one can be significant. Borrowers who focus only on the base payment may underestimate the true monthly obligation and unintentionally stretch themselves too thin.

Cash reserves play a critical role in long-term stability. Borrowers who choose to borrow the maximum amount often deplete savings to meet down payment and closing cost requirements. While FHA allows low down payments, borrowers can still strain themselves by selecting a higher-priced home that requires every available dollar. This chapter emphasizes that liquidity is a form of security. Having reserves after closing provides peace of mind and flexibility, especially during the first year of ownership when unexpected expenses are most common.

Interest rates also affect the decision to borrow less than the maximum. A slightly lower loan amount can reduce the impact of future rate fluctuations, refinancing costs, and long-term interest expense. Borrowers who plan strategically often choose a home that allows them to qualify comfortably while preserving options for future upgrades, investments, or refinances. FHA loans make these choices possible by offering flexibility without penalty.

Lifestyle considerations matter as much as financial ones. A mortgage payment that leaves no room for travel, education, childcare, or emergency savings can quietly erode the benefits of ownership. FHA borrowers who choose a payment aligned with their lifestyle goals tend to remain homeowners longer and experience less stress. This chapter reframes affordability as a personal decision rather than a lender-imposed limit.

Another key concept introduced here is future-proofing. Borrowers should consider potential changes in income, family size, or employment stability. FHA loans are forgiving, but life is unpredictable. Borrowers who leave margin in their budget are better prepared to weather transitions without panic or forced decisions. The strongest FHA borrowers are not those who stretch the furthest, but those who plan the smartest.

This chapter reinforces that FHA loans are tools for stability, not tests of endurance. Choosing to borrow less than the maximum is not a sign of weakness; it is a sign of foresight. When borrowers align approval with comfort, they turn homeownership into a platform for growth rather than a source of pressure. FHA makes this balance achievable for borrowers who understand that the best loan is the one that supports both today's needs and tomorrow's goals.

"Samantha Left Room to Breathe"

Samantha was approved for an FHA loan up to $420,000. When she received the preapproval letter, she felt proud and relieved. But as she started browsing homes, she noticed something unsettling. Every time she looked at properties near the top of her approval range, the monthly payment felt tight. Instead of ignoring that feeling, Samantha decided to run the numbers carefully.

At $420,000 with a 3.5 percent down payment, her down payment would be $14,700, leaving a loan amount of $405,300. Her estimated monthly payment, including mortgage insurance, taxes, and insurance, came out to about $2,950. That number fit within her approved debt ratios, but it left little room for savings or unexpected expenses.

Samantha then looked at homes priced around $360,000. Her down payment at 3.5 percent would be $12,600, resulting in a loan amount of $347,400. Her estimated monthly payment dropped to around $2,500. The difference was roughly $450 per month. Over a year, that amounted to $5,400.

Samantha compared the two scenarios side by side. By choosing the lower-priced home, she saved $2,100 upfront on her down payment and $5,400 per year in monthly cash flow. Over five years, that was $27,000 in preserved income, not including interest savings. That money could fund emergencies, vacations, or future investments.

On closing day, Samantha felt confident instead of stretched. Her home met her needs, her payment felt manageable, and her savings account remained intact. FHA hadn't pushed her to the maximum. It had given her the freedom to choose what truly fit.

Chapter 6

Putting It All Together — Turning FHA Rules into a Confident Buying Strategy

By the time a borrower reaches this stage of understanding FHA loan limits, down payments, closing costs, and approval ranges, something important has shifted. The process no longer feels like a collection of confusing rules imposed by lenders. Instead, it begins to resemble a system—one that can be understood, planned for, and used intentionally. This chapter exists to connect all of the individual components discussed so far into a single, coherent strategy. FHA loans are not meant to be navigated piece by piece in isolation. Their true value is revealed when borrowers see how each rule interacts with the others and how thoughtful planning can dramatically improve both the buying experience and the long-term outcome.

The first step in building a confident FHA buying strategy is understanding that every number in the transaction influences at least one other number. Loan limits define the outer boundaries of possibility, but income and debt ratios determine what portion of that boundary is reachable. Down payments reduce loan amounts, which in turn affect monthly payments, mortgage insurance, and interest expense. Closing costs influence how much cash is required at the table, which impacts reserves and post-closing stability. When borrowers view these elements together rather than separately, decision-making becomes clearer and more intentional.

A strategic FHA borrower begins by defining comfort, not maximums. Instead of asking how much they can borrow, they ask how much they want their housing payment to be relative to their lifestyle and future goals. This personal benchmark then informs the price range they shop in, the property types they consider, and the level of seller concessions they negotiate. FHA guidelines provide flexibility, but strategy gives that flexibility direction. Without strategy, borrowers risk drifting toward the highest allowable numbers simply because they are available.

Cash management is the second pillar of a strong FHA strategy. FHA allows low down payments and flexible closing cost structures for a reason: preserving liquidity supports sustainable ownership. Borrowers who intentionally structure their deals to keep cash reserves often experience less stress and greater confidence after closing. This does not mean avoiding responsibility or underestimating costs. It means planning for them without overcommitting upfront. FHA's design acknowledges that ownership extends beyond the closing date, and strategy must as well. Negotiation is another area where FHA strategy matters. Borrowers who understand seller contributions, lender credits, and pricing tradeoffs negotiate differently than those who focus only on purchase price. They view the transaction holistically, balancing price, credits, and long-term payment impact. This approach often results in deals that are financially healthier, even if they appear slightly higher on paper. FHA borrowers who master this mindset stop reacting to numbers and start shaping them.

Risk management is also a critical part of FHA strategy. Life is unpredictable, and even the most stable borrowers face changes in income, expenses, or family needs. FHA loans include safeguards such as flexible credit standards and refinance options, but borrowers who leave margin in their budgets are better prepared to use those safeguards if needed. Strategy means planning not just for the ideal scenario, but for resilience when conditions change.

Another important element is forward thinking. FHA loans are often a starting point, not an endpoint. Borrowers may plan to refinance, move, or leverage equity in the future. Choosing the right loan size, payment, and cash structure today can make those future moves easier and more profitable. A strategic FHA borrower does not view the loan as a static obligation, but as a dynamic tool that can evolve over time.

This chapter reinforces that FHA success is not about gaming the system or pushing boundaries. It is about alignment. When loan limits, down payments, closing costs, and personal goals are aligned, the process feels predictable rather than stressful. Borrowers move from uncertainty to clarity, from hesitation to confidence. FHA provides the framework, but strategy turns that framework into results.

Ultimately, this chapter brings the reader full circle. The numbers that once felt intimidating now feel familiar. The rules that once felt restrictive now feel supportive. FHA loans become not just a way to buy a home, but a platform for stability and growth. With understanding and intention, borrowers can step into homeownership not as hopeful applicants, but as confident decision-makers.

"The Plan That Finally Made Sense"

Nicole and James had been approved for an FHA loan of up to $460,000, but instead of celebrating, they felt overwhelmed. Every decision seemed heavy, and every number felt final. Instead of rushing forward, they decided to create a plan. They started by deciding what monthly payment felt comfortable. After reviewing their budget, they chose $2,600 as a number that allowed room for savings, travel, and emergencies.

They worked backward from that payment and discovered it aligned with a purchase price of about $385,000. At that price, their FHA down payment at 3.5 percent would be $13,475. Their estimated loan amount would be $371,525. Closing costs were estimated at $11,000, but they planned to negotiate seller contributions to cover most of that amount.

Nicole and James compared this plan to buying at the top of their approval range. At $460,000, their down payment would have been $16,100, their payment closer to $3,100 per month, and their savings nearly depleted. Over a year, the payment difference between the two scenarios was about $6,000. Over five years, it exceeded $30,000.

By choosing strategy over maximums, Nicole and James closed with money in the bank and confidence in their decision. The numbers worked together instead of against them. FHA didn't limit their options. It gave them a structure they could finally trust.

Chapter 7

Thinking Two Moves Ahead — Using FHA Today Without Limiting Tomorrow

One of the greatest mistakes borrowers make with FHA loans is treating the purchase as the final destination instead of the first strategic move. FHA financing is often viewed as a stepping stone, but too many borrowers step onto it without looking ahead. They focus entirely on qualifying, closing, and moving in, without considering how today's decisions will affect refinancing options, equity growth, or future buying power. This chapter exists to shift the borrower's mindset from short-term approval to long-term positioning. FHA loans are most powerful when they are used with foresight.

Every decision made during the purchase phase carries long-term consequences. The price paid, the loan amount chosen, the cash preserved or depleted, and the structure of closing costs all influence what options will be available in the future. Borrowers who stretch to the maximum may succeed in closing, but they often find themselves boxed in later, unable to refinance easily, access equity comfortably, or move without financial stress. FHA allows flexibility, but flexibility without strategy can quietly become limitation. Equity growth is one of the most misunderstood elements of FHA planning. Many borrowers assume equity is created only through large down payments or rapid appreciation. In reality, equity grows through a combination of market movement, principal reduction, and smart purchase decisions. Buying below maximum affordability, preserving cash, and maintaining payment comfort allow borrowers to hold their homes longer and weather market cycles more effectively. FHA borrowers who plan for longevity often build equity more reliably than those who chase the largest possible purchase.

Refinancing is another future move that should be considered early. FHA loans come with mortgage insurance that lasts for a set period or, in some cases, for the life of the loan. Borrowers who understand this can plan exit strategies in advance. Choosing a loan amount that allows future refinancing into a conventional loan when equity reaches the required threshold can save tens of thousands of dollars over time. That opportunity depends on decisions made at purchase, not years later.

Cash preservation also plays a role in future flexibility. Borrowers who empty savings at closing may feel accomplished, but they often lack the resources needed to take advantage of future opportunities. Whether it is a refinance, a move-up purchase, or an unexpected investment opportunity, liquidity creates options. FHA's structure allows borrowers to enter ownership without sacrificing this flexibility, but only if they choose to use it that way.

Another long-term consideration is mobility. Life changes. Careers shift, families grow, and priorities evolve. Borrowers who buy at the edge of affordability often feel trapped by their payment, unable to sell, rent, or refinance without stress. FHA borrowers who leave margin in their budget are more adaptable. They can respond to change rather than react to pressure. Thinking two moves ahead transforms FHA from a temporary solution into a foundation for future decisions.

This chapter also reinforces the idea that FHA is not a downgrade from conventional financing. It is a different structure designed for accessibility and flexibility. Borrowers who use FHA intentionally often transition smoothly into other loan types later, carrying forward the stability they built early on. FHA becomes the starting chapter in a longer financial story rather than a detour.

Ultimately, this chapter invites borrowers to see FHA not just as a way to buy a home, but as a way to position themselves. The strongest FHA borrowers are not those who rush to close, but those who pause to plan. When today's decisions support tomorrow's goals, homeownership becomes empowering instead of restrictive. FHA provides the access. Strategy provides the future.

"Ethan Left the Door Open"

Ethan bought his first home with FHA at $330,000. His down payment at 3.5 percent was $11,550, and his loan amount came out to $318,450. He could have bought closer to $400,000, but he chose not to. His monthly payment landed at $2,200, well within his comfort zone. More importantly, he kept over $20,000 in savings after closing.

Five years later, Ethan reviewed his situation. His home had appreciated to $395,000. Over that time, he had paid down his loan balance to approximately $300,000. His equity was now about $95,000. He did the math. That equity represented roughly 24 percent of the home's value.

Because he had planned ahead, Ethan qualified to refinance into a conventional loan and remove mortgage insurance. His new payment dropped by nearly $250 per month. Over the next ten years, that savings would total $30,000. If Ethan had stretched to the maximum at purchase, the numbers would have looked very different.

Ethan compared his situation to a hypothetical alternative. If he had bought at $400,000, his down payment would have been $14,000, his payment closer to $2,750, and his ability to save each month reduced. Even with appreciation, his loan balance would have been higher, delaying refinancing and increasing total interest paid.

By choosing FHA strategically instead of emotionally, Ethan left the door open. The math rewarded patience. FHA didn't hold him back. It gave him the room to move forward when the time was right.

Chapter 8

When the Numbers Shift – Stress-Testing Your FHA Loan Before Life Does

One of the most overlooked steps in the FHA homebuying process is asking a simple but powerful question: what happens if the numbers change? Many borrowers approach their FHA loan as if the figures at closing will remain static for decades. In reality, life is dynamic. Expenses rise, incomes fluctuate, families grow, and priorities evolve. FHA loans are built to be flexible, but that flexibility is most effective when borrowers proactively test their financial structure against change rather than reacting to it after the fact. This chapter introduces the concept of stress-testing an FHA loan before closing, ensuring that ownership remains sustainable even when circumstances shift.

Stress-testing does not mean assuming worst-case scenarios or expecting failure. It means evaluating how resilient the loan structure is under reasonable variations. What if property taxes increase? What if insurance premiums rise? What if one income is temporarily reduced? FHA borrowers who account for these possibilities early are better prepared to absorb them calmly. This chapter reframes preparation as empowerment, not pessimism.

The first variable to examine is monthly housing cost. FHA payments include principal, interest, mortgage insurance, taxes, and insurance. While principal and interest remain fixed in a fixed-rate loan, the other components can change. Property taxes are reassessed, insurance costs fluctuate, and mortgage insurance remains in place for a defined period. Borrowers who budget only for the initial payment may be surprised later. Stress-testing involves asking whether the payment remains manageable if these components increase modestly over time.

Income stability is another critical factor. FHA allows borrowers to qualify using current, verifiable income, but life does not always follow linear paths. Career transitions, business cycles, parental leave, or health events can affect earnings. Borrowers who rely on every dollar of current income to support their payment leave themselves little margin. FHA's flexible guidelines allow borrowers to qualify, but strategy requires them to leave room. This chapter encourages borrowers to evaluate how the payment feels under reduced income scenarios, not just ideal ones.

Cash reserves serve as the shock absorbers in any financial plan. FHA does not require large reserves for most owner-occupied purchases, but that does not mean reserves are unimportant. Borrowers who preserve savings at closing are better positioned to handle repairs, temporary income changes, or unexpected expenses without stress. Stress-testing includes evaluating how long reserves could sustain the household if income dipped or expenses rose. This exercise often leads borrowers to adjust purchase price, down payment strategy, or closing cost structure before it is too late.

Another aspect of stress-testing involves future interest rate environments. While FHA fixed-rate loans provide stability, refinancing opportunities depend on equity, credit, and market conditions. Borrowers who stretch to the maximum may find themselves unable to refinance when rates drop or when they want to remove mortgage insurance. Stress-testing includes considering whether the loan structure allows flexibility for future adjustments, not just current affordability.

Lifestyle resilience also matters. A mortgage payment that technically fits may still crowd out other important areas of life such as education, travel, healthcare, or family support. FHA borrowers who stress-test their budgets often discover that a slightly lower purchase price creates disproportionate relief. This chapter emphasizes that sustainability is not about sacrifice; it is about balance. The goal of stress-testing is not to discourage ownership, but to strengthen it. FHA loans are designed to support borrowers through different stages of life, but the borrower must choose a structure that aligns with that journey. When borrowers test their numbers honestly, they often gain confidence rather than doubt. They move forward knowing that their loan can withstand reasonable change.

This chapter reinforces that the strongest FHA loan is not the one that barely works on paper, but the one that continues to work when life introduces variables. Stress-testing transforms FHA from a qualifying exercise into a long-term strategy. Borrowers who do this work before closing rarely regret it afterward.

"The Payment That Could Breathe"

Lauren and Michael were approved for an FHA loan up to $440,000. At first, they focused on homes priced around $415,000. Their estimated monthly payment was $3,050. The number worked based on their combined income, but something felt tight. Instead of ignoring the feeling, they decided to stress-test the numbers.

They started by adjusting property taxes upward by $200 per month to account for reassessment. The payment rose to $3,250. Next, they imagined a temporary income reduction. If one of them lost $1,000 per month for six months, the payment would suddenly consume a much larger portion of their remaining income. The math made them uneasy.

They ran a second scenario using a purchase price of $365,000. Their down payment at 3.5 percent was $12,775, and their payment came in around $2,650. Even with a $200 tax increase, the payment stayed under $2,850. The difference between the two scenarios was about $400 per month.

Lauren calculated the annual impact. Four hundred dollars per month was $4,800 per year. Over five years, that was $24,000 in breathing room. They compared that number to their savings and realized that the lower-priced home allowed them to keep over $10,000 more in reserves after closing.

When they closed, Lauren and Michael felt prepared rather than stretched. A year later, when insurance premiums increased and Michael took unpaid leave to care for a family member, their budget absorbed the change without panic. The payment could breathe. FHA didn't just help them buy a home. It helped them stay in it.

Chapter 9

The Hidden Math of Long-Term Cost – What FHA Borrowers Pay Over Time, Not Just Today

Most FHA borrowers focus intensely on the numbers required to get into a home: the down payment, the closing costs, and the initial monthly payment. While these figures are important, they represent only the beginning of the financial story. The true cost of homeownership unfolds over years, not days. FHA loans are often criticized for mortgage insurance and perceived higher long-term expense, but these critiques are frequently based on incomplete math. This chapter explores the full financial arc of an FHA loan, helping borrowers understand what they truly pay over time and how smart decisions at purchase can dramatically change that outcome.

Mortgage insurance is one of the most misunderstood elements of FHA financing. FHA requires both an upfront mortgage insurance premium and an annual premium paid monthly. Many borrowers hear this and assume FHA is automatically more expensive than other loan options. What is often missed is context. Mortgage insurance exists to allow lower down payments, flexible credit, and broader access to ownership. The question is not whether mortgage insurance exists, but how long it remains, how much it costs relative to alternatives, and what it enables the borrower to do with their cash and credit in the meantime.

The upfront mortgage insurance premium is typically financed into the loan, increasing the loan balance slightly. While this raises the amount borrowed, spreading the cost over the life of the loan minimizes its immediate impact. Borrowers who compare this to bringing additional cash to closing often find that financing the premium preserves liquidity and reduces financial stress early on. Over time, the cost becomes part of the larger loan structure rather than an upfront burden.

The annual mortgage insurance premium is paid monthly and varies based on loan amount and loan-to-value ratio. This cost does increase the monthly payment, but it must be evaluated in comparison to alternatives. Conventional loans with low down payments often include private mortgage insurance that can be similar or even higher in cost, especially for borrowers with average credit. FHA mortgage insurance also provides stability, as it does not fluctuate based on credit score after closing.

Long-term cost analysis also includes interest paid over time. Borrowers who choose higher loan amounts or longer loan terms will pay more interest overall. However, the difference between FHA and conventional interest rates can vary widely depending on market conditions and borrower profile. FHA often offers competitive rates for borrowers who would otherwise face higher costs elsewhere. The key is not the label on the loan, but how the numbers align with the borrower's strategy.

This chapter emphasizes that total cost is shaped less by the loan program and more by borrower behavior. Borrowers who refinance when appropriate, pay extra toward principal when possible, or move strategically often reduce total cost significantly. FHA loans do not trap borrowers into permanent expense. They provide entry and flexibility. The long-term outcome depends on how the borrower uses that flexibility.

Time is another factor that changes the math. Borrowers who stay in a home for three to five years experience a different cost profile than those who remain for decades. FHA loans are particularly effective for borrowers who plan to refinance or move within a defined timeframe, as the benefits of low entry cost can outweigh the cumulative insurance expense. Understanding time horizon allows borrowers to evaluate FHA realistically rather than emotionally.

This chapter also addresses the psychological cost of ownership. Financial stress, depleted savings, and lack of flexibility can be more damaging than modest insurance premiums. FHA borrowers who preserve cash, maintain reserves, and structure manageable payments often experience a better quality of ownership, even if the loan carries additional costs on paper. The math must account for stability, not just totals.

Ultimately, this chapter reframes FHA cost as dynamic rather than fixed. What a borrower pays over time depends on decisions made at purchase, actions taken after closing, and opportunities seized along the way. FHA loans are not inherently expensive or cheap. They are tools. When used intentionally, they often cost less than the alternatives borrowers assume they must accept. Understanding this long-term math transforms FHA from a temporary compromise into a strategic choice.

"The Five-Year Calculation That Changed Everything"

Jordan was hesitant about FHA because of mortgage insurance. Friends warned him that it would cost him tens of thousands of dollars over time. Instead of accepting the advice blindly, Jordan decided to calculate his actual scenario. He planned to stay in his home for about five years before upgrading.

Jordan purchased a home for $345,000 with a 3.5 percent down payment of $12,075. His base loan amount was $332,925, and his upfront mortgage insurance premium of 1.75 percent added $5,826 to the loan. His total loan balance became $338,751. His monthly mortgage insurance payment was approximately $235.

Jordan multiplied $235 by 60 months. Over five years, he would pay about $14,100 in mortgage insurance. Combined with the financed upfront premium, his total FHA insurance cost over five years was roughly $19,926.

Jordan then compared this to a conventional loan alternative. To avoid private mortgage insurance, he would have needed to put 20 percent down, or $69,000. That was $56,925 more cash upfront than FHA required. He calculated the opportunity cost. If he invested or saved that $56,925 instead, even modest returns would outweigh the insurance cost.

Five years later, Jordan's home had appreciated to $405,000, and his loan balance had dropped to about $315,000. His equity was now approximately $90,000. He refinanced into a conventional loan and eliminated mortgage insurance entirely.

When Jordan reviewed the numbers, the outcome surprised him. FHA had not cost him more. It had allowed him to buy earlier, preserve cash, and build equity faster than waiting.

The math was clear. FHA wasn't expensive. Waiting would have been.

Chapter 10

From Numbers to Confidence — How FHA Turns Knowledge into Ownership Power

By the time a borrower reaches the end of this book, the FHA loan is no longer a mystery made up of scattered rules and intimidating figures. The numbers that once felt abstract—loan limits, down payments, closing costs, mortgage insurance, and monthly obligations—now tell a story. That story is not about restriction, but about structure. FHA loans are designed to guide borrowers into homeownership with balance, not bravado, and with sustainability, not strain. This final chapter exists to solidify that understanding and to transform knowledge into confidence.

Confidence in homeownership does not come from approval letters or online calculators. It comes from understanding how the pieces fit together and knowing why a decision makes sense beyond the moment it is made. FHA borrowers who reach this level of clarity approach the process differently. They are no longer asking whether they qualify. They are deciding how they want to qualify and on what terms. This shift in mindset marks the transition from applicant to owner.

One of the most important lessons of FHA financing is that numbers are not adversaries. They are signals. Loan limits signal boundaries that protect borrowers from overextension. Down payment requirements signal entry points that preserve liquidity. Closing costs signal the true mechanics of ownership transfer. Mortgage insurance signals shared risk in exchange for access. When borrowers learn to interpret these signals instead of fearing them, the process becomes collaborative rather than confrontational.

This chapter reinforces that FHA loans are not about doing the minimum; they are about doing what works. FHA does not reward recklessness, nor does it punish caution. It provides a framework that adapts to the borrower's choices. Borrowers who choose balance experience stability. Borrowers who choose strategy experience flexibility. Borrowers who choose foresight experience opportunity. FHA does not dictate outcomes. It responds to intention.

Another core takeaway is that homeownership is not a single transaction, but a sequence of decisions over time. The purchase is only the first decision. Refinancing, upgrading, investing, or leveraging equity are future decisions influenced by today's structure. Borrowers who understand this avoid the trap of optimizing only for closing day. They optimize for the years that follow. FHA loans, when used thoughtfully, support this long-term view better than many borrowers expect.

This chapter also emphasizes personal alignment. No two borrowers have identical goals, incomes, or risk tolerances. FHA's flexibility allows borrowers to customize their path without violating guidelines. Some prioritize low cash at closing. Others prioritize lower monthly payments. Some plan to refinance quickly. Others plan to stay long-term. FHA accommodates all of these paths when borrowers understand the rules well enough to choose intentionally.

Fear often comes from uncertainty, and uncertainty comes from lack of understanding. By replacing fear with clarity, FHA borrowers gain leverage—not just financial leverage, but emotional leverage. They negotiate better, plan better, and sleep better after closing. Confidence is not arrogance. It is preparedness.

As this book concludes, the most important message is not about any single rule or calculation. It is about agency. FHA loans give borrowers agency when they understand them. The borrower who knows how loan limits work shops smarter. The borrower who understands down payments preserves cash wisely. The borrower who plans for closing costs avoids surprises. The borrower who understands long-term cost chooses the right time to refinance or move. Knowledge compounds, just like equity.

This final chapter invites borrowers to step forward with ownership, not hesitation. FHA is not a fallback plan. It is a deliberate choice for borrowers who value access, structure, and sustainability. When numbers are understood, they stop being obstacles and start becoming tools. That is the real power of FHA, and it is the power that turns knowledge into confident, lasting homeownership.

"The Decision That Felt Easy for Once"

Rebecca had waited years to buy a home because every time she ran the numbers, something felt unclear. This time was different. She had done the work. She knew the FHA loan limit in her county was well above her target price. She understood that her down payment at 3.5 percent on a $355,000 home would be $12,425. She knew her estimated closing costs were $10,500, and she planned to negotiate seller credits to cover most of them.

Rebecca calculated her loan amount after down payment as $342,575. With the financed upfront mortgage insurance premium added, her total loan balance was approximately $348,600. Her monthly payment, including mortgage insurance, taxes, and insurance, came out to $2,520. She compared that number to her monthly income and savings goals and confirmed it left room to breathe.

She ran a second scenario out of curiosity. If she bought at $415,000, still within approval, her down payment would increase to $14,525, her payment would rise to about $2,950, and her reserves would shrink. The difference between the two payments was $430 per month. Over a year, that was $5,160. Over five years, it exceeded $25,000.

Rebecca didn't hesitate. She chose the home that aligned with her life, not the maximum the bank allowed. On closing day, there were no surprises. The numbers matched her expectations. She left the table with keys, confidence, and savings still in the bank.

For the first time, buying a home didn't feel like a leap of faith. It felt like a decision backed by math. FHA didn't push her forward. It gave her the clarity to step forward on her own.

Chapter 11

The Borrower Advantage — How Informed FHA Buyers Control the Process Instead of Being Carried by It

There is a moment in every FHA transaction when the borrower either takes control or quietly hands it over. That moment is not at closing, and it is not even at preapproval. It happens much earlier, when the borrower decides whether they will understand the process deeply enough to guide it or simply react to it as it unfolds. FHA loans are often described as flexible, but flexibility alone does not create advantage. Advantage comes from understanding how and when to apply that flexibility. This chapter is about transforming FHA knowledge into borrower leverage.

Most borrowers enter the homebuying process assuming that lenders, agents, and underwriters are the sole decision-makers. While these professionals play critical roles, the borrower who understands FHA rules becomes an active participant rather than a passive recipient. When borrowers know how loan limits, down payments, and closing costs interact, they stop being surprised by numbers and start anticipating them. This shift changes the tone of every conversation. Questions become sharper. Decisions become faster. Anxiety gives way to certainty.

One of the greatest advantages an informed FHA borrower has is timing control. Understanding FHA mechanics allows borrowers to decide when to lock rates, when to negotiate credits, and when to walk away from deals that do not align with their strategy. Uninformed borrowers often feel rushed because they do not know which decisions matter most. Informed borrowers know where flexibility exists and where it does not. They do not panic at minor changes because they understand the system's margins.

Another powerful advantage is communication clarity. FHA transactions involve many moving parts, and confusion often arises not from complexity but from miscommunication. Borrowers who understand the numbers can identify discrepancies early, ask for clarification confidently, and prevent small issues from becoming major delays. They recognize when a fee seems out of place, when an estimate should be updated, or when a negotiation opportunity has been missed. This level of engagement does not create friction; it creates efficiency.

Control also comes from understanding tradeoffs. FHA borrowers who grasp how interest rates, lender credits, and seller concessions interact can make decisions that align with their priorities instead of defaulting to standard options. They understand that every choice has a cost and a benefit, and they evaluate those tradeoffs intentionally. This is the difference between accepting a loan and designing one.

This chapter also emphasizes that informed borrowers reduce risk for everyone involved. Lenders prefer borrowers who understand documentation requirements and timelines. Agents prefer clients who know how financing affects negotiations. Sellers prefer buyers who can close without surprises. Knowledge does not slow the process; it stabilizes it. FHA borrowers who understand the system often experience smoother transactions precisely because fewer issues catch them off guard.

Another often-overlooked advantage is emotional control. Real estate transactions are emotional by nature, and fear can lead to poor decisions. Borrowers who understand the numbers are less likely to overreact to changes in estimates, appraisal outcomes, or market conditions. They know what matters and what does not. This calm confidence protects them from making rushed concessions or abandoning good deals unnecessarily.

This chapter also reframes responsibility. FHA does not remove responsibility from the borrower; it redistributes it. The borrower is responsible for choosing how much to borrow, how much cash to deploy, and how much risk to accept. FHA provides guardrails, but the borrower steers. Those who understand this do not feel controlled by the process. They feel supported by it.

Ultimately, this chapter reinforces that FHA loans reward preparation. The borrower who understands FHA rules does not need to outsmart the system. They simply need to work with it deliberately. When borrowers control their numbers, they control their experience. That is the true borrower advantage, and it is available to anyone willing to learn how the system actually works.

"Anthony Read the Loan Estimate Differently"

Anthony had already been through one failed home purchase, and he wasn't about to repeat the experience. This time, he approached FHA differently. When he received his Loan Estimate for a $372,000 home, he didn't just look at the bottom line. He examined how the numbers were built.

His down payment at 3.5 percent was $13,020. His estimated closing costs were listed at $11,400. Anthony noticed that $4,200 of that amount was prepaid items, not true costs. That meant the transactional costs were closer to $7,200. He also noticed that the seller credit negotiated was only $5,000, leaving a shortfall.

Anthony ran the math. If the seller increased the credit to $7,200, his cash at closing would drop by $2,200. He calculated that increasing the purchase price by $2,200 would raise his monthly payment by less than $15. Over a year, that was $180. Over ten years, it was $1,800. He compared that to the $2,200 he would preserve immediately.

Anthony requested a contract amendment. The seller agreed. The updated Loan Estimate reflected the change exactly as expected. Nothing felt chaotic. Nothing felt uncertain. The numbers behaved the way they should when they were understood.

At closing, Anthony brought less cash than originally projected and still retained over $17,000 in savings. For the first time, the process felt controlled. FHA didn't make the deal work. Understanding FHA did.

Chapter 12

Owning the Outcome — How FHA Borrowers Turn One Home into Long-Term Wealth

The final evolution of an FHA borrower does not occur at closing, refinancing, or even when mortgage insurance is removed. It occurs when the borrower begins to understand that a home is not just a place to live, but a financial position that can be shaped, protected, and leveraged over time. FHA loans are often framed as entry-level tools, but borrowers who stop thinking at entry leave much of their potential unrealized. This chapter is about ownership of outcome—how informed FHA borrowers move beyond simply having a mortgage and begin using their home as a stable foundation for long-term wealth.

Wealth building through homeownership does not require speculation, extreme leverage, or rapid appreciation. It begins with structure. The purchase price chosen, the loan amount accepted, the cash preserved, and the payment comfort established all determine how resilient the ownership experience will be. FHA borrowers who buy within comfort rather than maximums often hold their homes longer, maintain them better, and experience fewer forced decisions. Stability, not speed, is what allows equity to accumulate naturally.

Equity grows in quiet ways that are often underestimated. Every monthly payment reduces principal. Every year of ownership shifts the loan-to-value ratio. Even modest appreciation compounds over time when paired with principal reduction. FHA borrowers who remain in their homes long enough often find that equity builds faster than expected, particularly when they avoid overextending early on. This chapter reinforces that wealth creation does not require dramatic moves; it requires patience and alignment.

Another key aspect of owning the outcome is understanding optionality. Borrowers who preserve cash and maintain manageable payments retain the ability to make choices. They can refinance when rates improve. They can tap equity strategically. They can move, rent, or upgrade without panic. FHA loans, when structured intentionally, create options instead of obligations. This is especially important for borrowers whose lives may change in unpredictable ways over time.

This chapter also reframes FHA mortgage insurance as temporary context rather than permanent cost. For borrowers who plan ahead, FHA insurance becomes a bridge rather than a burden. Whether the plan is to refinance into a conventional loan, sell and upgrade, or leverage equity for another purchase, the FHA loan serves its purpose during the early years when access matters most. The long-term outcome is shaped not by the presence of mortgage insurance, but by how long the borrower carries it and what they do during that time.

Ownership also brings responsibility, and responsibility brings opportunity. Borrowers who understand maintenance, budgeting, and long-term planning protect their equity rather than eroding it. FHA borrowers who keep reserves, invest in upkeep, and avoid reactive decisions tend to see their homes appreciate not just in market value, but in functional value. A well-maintained home supports refinancing, resale, and rental options far better than one neglected due to financial strain.

This chapter emphasizes that FHA loans do not cap ambition. They simply structure the beginning. Borrowers who treat FHA as a dead end often remain stuck, while those who treat it as a foundation often move forward with confidence. Wealth is not created by loan type. It is created by behavior, timing, and informed decision-making. FHA supports these behaviors when borrowers understand the full arc of ownership.

As this chapter closes, the reader is encouraged to view their FHA-financed home not as a finished achievement, but as a living asset. The goal is not just to buy wisely, but to own wisely. FHA loans provide access. Understanding provides leverage. Together, they allow borrowers to own not just the home, but the outcome that follows.

"Five Years Changed the Equation"

Daniel purchased his first home using FHA at a price of $325,000. His down payment at 3.5 percent was $11,375, leaving a base loan amount of $313,625. With the financed upfront mortgage insurance premium added, his total loan balance was approximately $319,100. His monthly payment felt comfortable, and he intentionally avoided stretching to the maximum he was approved for.

Over the next five years, Daniel made consistent payments and kept his home well maintained. His loan balance dropped to approximately $298,000 through normal amortization. At the same time, the market appreciated modestly, and similar homes in his area were now selling for around $385,000. Daniel calculated his equity. The difference between the value and the loan balance was about $87,000.

Daniel compared this outcome to an alternative scenario he had considered at purchase. If he had bought at $395,000 instead, his initial down payment would have been $13,825, his payment would have been significantly higher, and his ability to save each month reduced. Even with appreciation, his loan balance after five years would have been closer to $360,000, leaving far less usable equity.

With $87,000 in equity, Daniel refinanced into a conventional loan and eliminated mortgage insurance. His monthly payment dropped by nearly $300. Over the next ten years, that reduction alone would save him more than $36,000. The FHA loan had done exactly what it was supposed to do—it got him in the door early, preserved his cash, and allowed time to work in his favor.

Daniel didn't feel lucky. He felt prepared. The math had been there all along. FHA didn't make him wealthy overnight. It gave him the structure to let time do the work.

Chapter 13

Avoiding the Quiet Mistakes — How FHA Borrowers Protect Their Wins After Closing

For many borrowers, closing on a home feels like the finish line. The paperwork is signed, the keys are handed over, and the long journey appears complete. In reality, closing is not the end of the FHA process; it is the beginning of a new phase where decisions continue to shape outcomes quietly over time. The most costly FHA mistakes are rarely dramatic or obvious. They are subtle, incremental, and often made with good intentions. This chapter exists to help borrowers recognize and avoid those quiet mistakes before they erode the advantages FHA financing provides.

One of the most common post-closing mistakes is lifestyle inflation driven by relief. After months of saving, budgeting, and stress, many borrowers feel an urge to reward themselves. New furniture, upgrades, subscriptions, and discretionary spending slowly increase monthly obligations. While none of these expenses seem dangerous individually, together they can narrow the margin that made the FHA loan sustainable in the first place. Borrowers who forget that their payment comfort was carefully chosen may unintentionally recreate the pressure they worked so hard to avoid.

Another frequent mistake is neglecting cash reserves once ownership begins. FHA allows borrowers to enter homeownership with minimal reserves, but long-term success often depends on rebuilding and maintaining them. Repairs, insurance increases, tax adjustments, and unexpected life events do not arrive with warnings. Borrowers who assume the hardest part is over sometimes delay rebuilding savings, leaving themselves exposed. This chapter emphasizes that reserves are not a temporary necessity; they are a permanent strategy.

Refinancing missteps also fall into the category of quiet mistakes. Borrowers sometimes refinance too early, too often, or without fully understanding the cost-benefit tradeoff. FHA borrowers may be tempted by small payment reductions that reset loan terms, add fees, or extend mortgage insurance unnecessarily. A refinance should always be evaluated using math rather than emotion. Understanding break-even points, term length, and long-term interest impact protects borrowers from decisions that feel helpful in the short term but costly over time.

Another subtle issue arises when borrowers misunderstand equity. Seeing rising home values can create a false sense of financial security. Equity is not cash, and accessing it always involves cost, risk, or obligation. FHA borrowers who rush to tap equity without a clear plan may weaken their position rather than strengthen it. This chapter encourages borrowers to view equity as a resource to be used intentionally, not casually.

Maintenance neglect is another quiet threat. Homes require ongoing care, and deferred maintenance can quickly become expensive. Borrowers who stretched financially at purchase may delay repairs, leading to larger costs later. FHA borrowers who preserved cash and budget margin are better equipped to maintain their homes, protect value, and support future refinancing or resale. Ownership success depends as much on stewardship as on financing.

This chapter also addresses mindset. Borrowers who see FHA as a temporary compromise may disengage from long-term planning, assuming they will "fix it later." Borrowers who see FHA as a strategic foundation remain engaged, informed, and proactive. The difference is not income or intelligence; it is intention. Quiet mistakes happen when attention fades.

Avoiding these mistakes does not require perfection. It

requires awareness. Borrowers who periodically revisit their numbers, reassess goals, and adjust behavior stay aligned with the strategy that got them into ownership successfully. FHA loans do not punish small missteps, but they reward consistency.

Ultimately, this chapter reinforces that FHA success is not determined at closing. It is determined by what borrowers do after the excitement fades. The borrowers who protect their wins are not those who obsess over every dollar, but those who remember why they structured their loan the way they did. When FHA borrowers stay intentional, the quiet years become the most powerful ones.

"What Michael Didn't Do Made the Difference"

Michael purchased his home using FHA for $310,000 with a 3.5 percent down payment of $10,850. His loan amount after adding the financed mortgage insurance premium was approximately $305,000. His monthly payment came in at $2,250, which fit comfortably within his budget. He had deliberately chosen not to buy at the top of his approval range.

During the first year, Michael resisted the urge to upgrade everything at once. Instead of financing new furniture, he set aside $400 per month into savings. At the end of the year, he had accumulated $4,800. When his property taxes increased by $120 per month the following year, the adjustment didn't disrupt his budget. The math had already accounted for margin. Three years in, Michael was approached about refinancing to reduce his payment by $90 per month. Instead of rushing forward, he calculated the cost. The refinance fees totaled $5,400. Dividing that by the monthly savings showed it would take five years just to break even. Since he planned to refinance again later to remove mortgage insurance, he declined. That decision alone saved him thousands.

Five years after purchase, Michael's home was worth approximately $375,000. His loan balance had dropped to about $285,000. His equity stood near $90,000. He refinanced once, removed mortgage insurance, and reduced his payment by $280 per month. Over ten years, that savings would exceed $33,000.

Michael never felt like he was doing something extraordinary. He simply avoided quiet mistakes. The math worked because he didn't work against it. FHA didn't just help him buy a home. It rewarded him for staying intentional long after the keys were handed over.

Chapter 14

The Calm Borrower Wins — Why FHA Rewards Patience, Planning, and Perspective

By the time most borrowers reach this point in their FHA journey, they have already learned how the rules work, how the numbers connect, and how to structure a deal that fits their life. What remains is not technical knowledge, but behavioral discipline. FHA loans quietly reward borrowers who remain calm, patient, and intentional over time. This chapter explores why the calm borrower consistently outperforms the anxious one, not because they are smarter or luckier, but because they allow the math to work without interference.

The FHA program is built on long-term averages, not short-term reactions. It assumes that borrowers will experience fluctuations in income, expenses, and markets, and it provides room for those fluctuations without forcing immediate consequences. Borrowers who understand this do not rush decisions when conditions shift slightly. They do not panic over temporary market changes, minor payment adjustments, or short-term uncertainty. They recognize that

FHA was designed to absorb normal life movement, not eliminate it. One of the most common sources of borrower anxiety is comparison. Borrowers often compare their FHA loan to someone else's conventional loan, someone else's interest rate, or someone else's purchase price. These comparisons are usually incomplete and misleading. FHA borrowers who remain calm understand that loan structure must match personal context. A lower rate elsewhere does not matter if it required excessive cash depletion or increased risk. FHA rewards borrowers who focus inward rather than outward.

Another reason calm borrowers win is that they allow equity to grow naturally. They do not rush to sell at the first sign of appreciation, nor do they panic during flat periods. FHA borrowers who hold steady through ordinary market cycles often experience stronger long-term outcomes than those who constantly reposition based on emotion. Equity is built through time and consistency, not constant action.

Patience also plays a role in refinancing decisions. Borrowers who react emotionally to every rate movement often refinance repeatedly, accumulating fees and resetting timelines. Calm FHA borrowers wait until refinancing clearly improves their position. They understand break-even math. They recognize when mortgage insurance removal, rate improvement, or term adjustment truly benefits them. This restraint preserves long-term savings that far exceed short-term excitement.

Planning reinforces calmness. Borrowers who enter ownership with reserves, payment margin, and realistic expectations experience fewer moments of panic. When expenses rise or life shifts, their response is measured rather than reactive. FHA loans support this stability, but only if borrowers choose not to override it with impulsive decisions. This chapter emphasizes that calmness is not passive; it is the result of preparation.

Perspective is the final element. FHA borrowers who succeed long-term understand that ownership is not about perfection. Homes require maintenance. Markets fluctuate. Payments adjust. None of these realities represent failure. They are part of ownership. Calm borrowers do not interpret normal challenges as signs they made a mistake. They interpret them as confirmation that planning matters.

This chapter reframes success not as maximizing returns, but as minimizing regret. Borrowers who remain calm rarely look back wishing they had stretched more, rushed faster, or chased trends. They look back grateful that they chose sustainability over spectacle. FHA rewards this mindset quietly, steadily, and predictably.

As this chapter closes, the reader is reminded that the FHA loan is not a test of nerve. It is a framework that works best when the borrower trusts it. Calm borrowers win because they allow time, math, and discipline to compound. In the end, FHA does not reward urgency. It rewards alignment.

"Nothing Happened — And That Was the Point"

Rachel bought her home using FHA for $340,000. Her down payment at 3.5 percent was $11,900, and her loan balance after financing the upfront mortgage insurance premium was approximately $334,000. Her monthly payment came in at $2,480, a number she chose carefully to leave margin.

Two years later, home values in her area rose quickly. Similar homes were selling for $390,000. Friends urged her to sell, refinance, or tap equity. Rachel did the math instead. Her loan balance had dropped to about $325,000. Her equity was roughly $65,000. If she refinanced immediately, she would incur $6,000 in costs and still carry mortgage insurance. The numbers didn't justify the move.

In year three, rates dropped slightly. Rachel was again encouraged to refinance. This time, the payment reduction would have been $85 per month. She calculated the break-even point. The refinance costs were $5,500. Dividing that by $85 showed it would take over five years to recover the cost. Since she planned to refinance later to remove mortgage insurance, she waited. Five years after purchase, Rachel's home was worth approximately $415,000. Her loan balance was around $300,000. Her equity was now $115,000. She refinanced into a conventional loan, eliminated mortgage insurance, and reduced her payment by $310 per month. Over ten years, that savings would exceed $37,000.

When Rachel looked back, nothing dramatic had happened. No risky moves. No rushed decisions. No emotional pivots. The math worked because she didn't interrupt it. FHA didn't reward action. It rewarded patience.

Chapter 15

The FHA Mindset Shift — When Borrowers Stop Chasing Approval and Start Designing Outcomes

The final transformation an FHA borrower undergoes has nothing to do with credit scores, income documentation, or even loan structure. It is a mental shift that quietly separates those who merely obtain homeownership from those who sustain and benefit from it over time. This shift occurs when borrowers stop chasing approval and start designing outcomes. FHA loans were never intended to be hurdles to clear; they were intended to be frameworks to work within. Borrowers who understand this stop reacting to the process and begin shaping it.

Approval-focused borrowers ask one primary question: will I get approved? Outcome-focused borrowers ask a different one: what do I want my ownership experience to look like? This difference may seem subtle, but it changes everything. When borrowers are fixated on approval, they tend to stretch numbers, deplete savings, and accept discomfort in exchange for access. When borrowers focus on outcomes, they evaluate how each decision affects stability, flexibility, and long-term well-being. FHA rewards the second mindset far more consistently than the first.

The FHA mindset shift begins with understanding that qualification is not a finish line. It is simply permission to choose. Once borrowers are approved, every major variable remains within their control: price, payment comfort, cash deployment, negotiation strategy, and future positioning. FHA does not force borrowers to borrow more, pay more, or risk more. It allows borrowers to choose those things if they wish. The power lies not in the rules, but in how the borrower applies them.

Another element of this mindset shift is redefining success. Many borrowers equate success with buying the most expensive home they can qualify for or achieving ownership as quickly as possible. FHA borrowers who thrive redefine success as sustainability. They value predictability over prestige, margin over maximums, and confidence over comparison. This redefinition allows them to experience ownership as an asset rather than a burden.

This chapter also addresses the temptation to override planning with emotion. The homebuying process is filled with emotional triggers—competition, fear of missing out, social pressure, and urgency. FHA borrowers who remain approval-focused are particularly vulnerable to these triggers because they believe approval is rare or fragile. Outcome-focused borrowers understand that FHA approval is a tool, not a gift. They trust their preparation enough to walk away from deals that do not align with their strategy.

Designing outcomes also means understanding that every FHA rule exists for a reason. Loan limits protect against overextension. Down payment structures preserve liquidity. Mortgage insurance spreads risk. Closing cost flexibility supports access. Borrowers who respect these design principles stop fighting the system and start benefiting from it. FHA works best when borrowers align with its intent rather than pushing against its edges.

This mindset shift also extends beyond the mortgage itself. Outcome-focused FHA borrowers think about how ownership fits into their broader life goals. They consider career flexibility, family needs, geographic mobility, and long-term financial plans. They understand that a home is not just a purchase, but a platform. FHA loans, when used intentionally, allow borrowers to step onto that platform without sacrificing future choices.

Another defining trait of outcome-focused borrowers is patience. They are not rushed by market noise or comparison.

They trust math over hype and planning over pressure. They allow time to work in their favor rather than attempting to force outcomes prematurely. FHA quietly rewards this patience through stability, equity growth, and optionality.

As this chapter closes, the reader is reminded that FHA loans do not determine outcomes—borrowers do. FHA provides access, structure, and flexibility. The borrower provides intention, discipline, and perspective. When these elements come together, homeownership stops being a goal achieved and becomes a strategy lived. The FHA mindset shift is not about thinking bigger. It is about thinking clearer.

"Approval Was Never the Goal"

Kevin was approved for an FHA loan up to $445,000, and at first, he treated that number like a trophy. It felt like validation. But before making an offer, Kevin paused and did something he had never done before—he designed the outcome he wanted. He decided he wanted a payment under $2,700, at least $15,000 in savings after closing, and flexibility to change jobs if needed.

Kevin ran the numbers. At $445,000, his down payment at 3.5 percent would be $15,575. His estimated payment would land around $3,050. His savings after closing would drop below $8,000. The numbers technically worked, but they didn't match the outcome he wanted. Kevin ran a second scenario at $370,000. His down payment would be $12,950. His loan balance after financing the upfront mortgage insurance premium would be approximately $363,000. His monthly payment would be about $2,560. After closing, he would still have over $18,000 in reserves. The difference in payment was nearly $500 per month.

Kevin multiplied $500 by twelve. That was $6,000 per year. Over five years, that difference would total $30,000. He compared that to the extra equity he might gain by buying higher and realized the tradeoff wasn't worth it. The math made the decision obvious.

Kevin chose the $370,000 home. At closing, nothing felt rushed. Nothing felt fragile. Two years later, when he accepted a new job with a temporary pay reduction but long-term upside, his payment remained comfortable. His savings stayed intact. His home supported his life instead of dictating it.

Kevin realized something important. Approval had never been the goal. Control was. FHA didn't limit his ambition. It gave him the structure to design an outcome that actually worked.

Final Thoughts

Homeownership is often described as a milestone, but in truth it is a mindset. The moment a borrower understands this, the entire experience changes. FHA loans are not merely financial products; they are frameworks built to support that mindset. Throughout this book, the goal has never been to overwhelm you with rules or numbers, but to replace uncertainty with understanding. When borrowers understand how FHA loan limits, down payments, and closing costs truly work, fear loses its grip. What remains is choice. Choice is the real privilege FHA offers, and it is the foundation of confident ownership.

Many borrowers enter the homebuying process believing the numbers are stacked against them. They assume the system is rigid, unforgiving, or designed only for those with perfect circumstances. FHA exists to counter that belief. It acknowledges that real people have real lives, varied incomes, imperfect credit histories, and evolving goals. FHA does not lower standards; it broadens access. The borrower who understands this stops asking whether they belong and starts deciding how they want to proceed.

This book has shown that loan limits are not barriers but boundaries meant to protect sustainability. They are not targets to hit, but guides to respect. Down payments are not tests of discipline, but tools for liquidity management. Closing costs are not hidden traps, but predictable components that can be planned for and negotiated. Mortgage insurance is not punishment, but shared risk that enables access. Each element serves a purpose. When seen together, they form a system that rewards preparation, patience, and intention.

One of the most important lessons of FHA financing is that the loudest voices in real estate are often the least helpful. Advice that encourages stretching, rushing, or chasing approval often ignores long-term consequences. FHA quietly favors borrowers who slow down, run the numbers, and think beyond the moment of closing. The most successful FHA borrowers are not those who maximize everything at once, but those who balance competing priorities thoughtfully.

Another theme woven throughout this book is margin. Margin is what allows life to happen without crisis. It is what allows you to absorb a tax increase, a repair, a career change, or a family shift without panic. FHA loans allow margin if borrowers choose to preserve it. The borrower who leaves room in their budget, keeps reserves, and avoids emotional decisions experiences ownership differently. The home becomes a support system, not a source of stress. It is also important to recognize that FHA is not a destination. It is a beginning. For some borrowers, it is a bridge to conventional financing. For others, it is a long-term solution that works beautifully. There is no single correct path. The only mistake is treating FHA as something to escape rather than something to use intentionally. Borrowers who respect the structure FHA provides often move forward more smoothly than those who fight against it.

Homeownership should not feel fragile. If a single expense, rate change, or market shift can undo the experience, something was misaligned at the start. FHA gives borrowers the opportunity to align financing with reality rather than aspiration alone. When that alignment exists, ownership becomes durable. Durable ownership is what builds equity, confidence, and opportunity over time.

This book has emphasized math not because numbers are everything, but because numbers tell the truth when emotions cannot. Math removes ego from decision-making. It reveals tradeoffs honestly. It clarifies what is gained and what is sacrificed. Borrowers who trust the math sleep better at night. They do not wonder whether they made a mistake. They know why they made the choice they did.

Perhaps the most important takeaway is this: FHA does not decide your outcome. You do. FHA provides access, flexibility, and structure. The outcome is shaped by how you use them. Borrowers who chase approval often feel relieved at closing but anxious afterward. Borrowers who design outcomes feel calm at closing and confident afterward. The difference is not income or intelligence. It is perspective.

As you move forward from this book, remember that homeownership is not a race. It is a long game. The goal is not to impress anyone, keep up with anyone, or prove anything. The goal is to create stability, optionality, and peace of mind. FHA loans were designed for that purpose. When used with understanding, they do exactly what they were meant to do.

In the end, the most successful FHA borrowers are not those who borrowed the most, paid the most, or rushed the fastest. They are the ones who understood the rules, respected the math, and trusted themselves enough to choose what fit. If this book has helped you do that, then it has done its job. The rest is yours to design.

The FHA Homeownership & Wealth Series

Complete Roadmap: From First-Time Buyer to Long-Term Wealth Builder

The FHA Homeownership & Wealth Series is designed as a progressive journey. Each book builds on the previous one, guiding borrowers from basic understanding to confident ownership, strategic financing, and long-term wealth creation. Readers can enter at any stage, but those who follow the full roadmap gain the clearest, fastest path to results.

This series is structured to meet borrowers exactly where they are—and show them what comes next.

Phase 1: Foundation & Confidence (Books 1–3)

Understanding FHA and realizing you qualify

These books eliminate confusion, fear, and misinformation. They are designed to answer the most important early question: *Is homeownership actually possible for me?*

Book 1 – FHA Loans Explained for Beginners How FHA Mortgages Work, Who Qualifies, and Why They're One of the Easiest Paths to Homeownership This is the foundation of the entire series. Readers learn how FHA loans work, why they exist, and how to evaluate FHA realistically using math instead of myths. This book builds confidence and replaces hesitation with clarity.

Book 2 – Buying Your First Home with FHA A Step-by-Step Guide to Purchasing a Home with Low Down Payment and Flexible Credit Rules This book turns understanding into action. Readers learn the full buying process—from pre-approval to closing—so they know exactly what to expect and how to avoid common first-time buyer mistakes.

Book 3 – FHA Loans for Borrowers with Low Credit or Past Credit Issues How to Get Approved with FHA Even with Late Payments, Collections, or a Low Credit Score This book is for borrowers who believe their credit disqualifies them. It explains FHA's second-chance philosophy and shows how recovery, not perfection, determines approval.

Phase 2: Income Reality & Property Flexibility (Books 4–6)

Qualifying with real-life finances and real homes

These books expand what readers believe is possible by addressing income types, property types, and cash requirements.

Book 4 – FHA Loans for Self-Employed, 1099 & Gig Workers How Business Owners and Independent

Contractors Qualify for FHA Home Loans This book demystifies income calculations for non-traditional earners and shows how FHA accommodates modern work patterns.

Book 5 – FHA Loans for Fixer-Uppers, Condos & Non-Perfect Homes How to Buy Homes That Need Repairs or Don't Fit Traditional Loan Guidelines Readers learn how FHA views property condition and how renovation and condo options expand buying opportunities.

Book 6 – FHA Loan Limits, Down Payment & Closing Costs How Much You Can Borrow and How to Bring Less Money to the Closing Table This book focuses on numbers. Readers learn how FHA loan limits work, how to reduce cash to close, and how seller credits and assistance programs change affordability.

Phase 3: Optimization & Refinancing Strategy (Books 7–8)

Using FHA beyond the purchase

These books show how FHA loans evolve with the borrower.

Book 7 – FHA Refinance Options Made Simple Streamline, Rate-and-Term, and Cash-Out Refinancing Explained for Homeowners Readers learn how FHA supports refinancing, payment reduction, and financial repositioning over time.

Book 8 – Using an FHA Cash-Out Refinance to Build Wealth How to Turn Home Equity into Cash Without Selling Your Home This book introduces equity as a strategic tool, not just a number on paper, while emphasizing responsible use.

Phase 4: Income & Expansion (Books 9–10)

Turning ownership into leverage

These books shift the reader from homeowner to strategist.

Book 9 – Buying Multi-Unit Homes with FHA How to Purchase 2–4 Unit Properties, Live in One, and Rent the Rest Readers learn how FHA enables owner-occupied investing and rent-offset strategies that dramatically reduce housing costs.

Book 10 – FHA Loan Myths, Mistakes & Borrower Strategies What Most Buyers Get Wrong—and How Smart Borrowers Win with FHA Loans This is the strategic wrap-up book that reinforces best practices, avoids costly errors, and helps readers think like informed borrowers.

About the Author

Joe Correa is a mortgage professional, educator, and financial strategist dedicated to helping everyday people understand homeownership, credit, and wealth-building without confusion or intimidation. With years of hands-on experience in the mortgage industry, Joe has worked with first-time buyers, self-employed borrowers, credit-challenged families, and aspiring investors who were often told "no" before learning what was actually possible.

What sets Joe apart is his ability to translate complex lending rules into clear, practical guidance. Rather than relying on theory, his work is grounded in real-world scenarios, real numbers, and real borrower outcomes. He believes that most people do not fail to buy homes because they lack income or discipline, but because they lack accurate information. His mission is to replace myths with math and fear with understanding.

Joe specializes in FHA loans because he has seen firsthand how transformative they can be when used correctly. He views FHA not as a last resort, but as one of the most powerful entry points into homeownership and long-term wealth—especially for borrowers navigating modern financial realities such as student loans, variable income, credit recovery, or limited savings. Through his writing, Joe teaches borrowers how to think strategically, act confidently, and use lending tools intentionally rather than emotionally.

In addition to his mortgage work, Joe is the creator of multiple educational programs and book series focused on homeownership, credit building, refinancing strategies, and financial independence. His approach emphasizes sustainability over speculation and progress over perfection. He is known for breaking down decisions into simple frameworks that empower readers to make smart choices at every stage of their journey.

Joe's writing style reflects his core belief: financial education should be accessible, practical, and empowering. He does not promise shortcuts or hype outcomes. Instead, he provides clarity, structure, and realistic paths forward—so readers can move from uncertainty to ownership with confidence.

When he is not writing or working with borrowers, Joe continues developing educational resources designed to help families build stability, equity, and long-term opportunity through informed financial decisions.

How to Get a Personalized FHA Review

If you found this book helpful, you may want to see how FHA loan options apply to your specific income, credit profile, cash to close, and homeownership goals.

Every borrower's situation is different. FHA guidelines, loan limits, interest rates, mortgage insurance, and available options vary based on income type, credit history, debt levels, savings, property type, and state guidelines. The examples in this book are educational, but your personal FHA eligibility, payment range, and strategy can only be determined through an individualized review.

As a licensed mortgage broker, I offer a **Personalized FHA Review** designed to show you: • Whether you currently qualify for an FHA loan • Your realistic home price and monthly payment range • How much cash you may need for down payment and closing costs • How credit, debt, or income factors affect your approval • Whether FHA is the best option for you now or later • What steps, if any, would strengthen your position

This review is fast, confidential, and focused entirely on helping you make informed homeownership decisions—without pressure or obligation.

To request your personalized FHA review, visit:https://finibimortgage.carrd.co/

You may also submit your information through the QR code provided in this book.

Your financial profile already tells a story.This review shows you how FHA lenders will read it.

Yours truly,

Joseph G. Correa

Licensed Mortgage Broker, Finibi Mortgage

Educational & Financial Disclaimer

This book is provided for educational and informational purposes only. The content is intended to help readers better understand FHA loans, homeownership concepts, and general mortgage strategies, but it does not constitute financial advice, legal advice, tax advice, or lending approval. Mortgage guidelines, FHA requirements, interest rates, loan programs, and qualification standards are subject to change and may vary based on individual circumstances, lender overlays, geographic location, and market conditions.

Nothing in this book should be interpreted as a guarantee of loan approval, loan terms, interest rates, or eligibility. All examples, scenarios, calculations, and illustrations are for educational purposes only and are not intended to represent actual loan offers or outcomes. Individual results will vary based on credit profile, income stability, debt obligations, assets, property characteristics, and lender-specific requirements.

Readers are encouraged to consult with a licensed mortgage professional, financial advisor, tax professional, or legal advisor before making any financial or real estate decisions. This book does not replace personalized advice or professional review. Any decisions made based on the information in this book are the sole responsibility of the reader.

The author and publisher are not responsible for any actions taken by readers as a result of the information provided in this book. While every effort has been made to ensure accuracy at the time of publication, no representation or warranty is made regarding the completeness, reliability, or current applicability of the information contained herein.

By reading this book, you acknowledge that homeownership and mortgage decisions involve risk and personal responsibility, and you agree that the author and publisher are not liable for any financial outcomes, losses, or damages that may result from reliance on this material.

This book is designed to educate, not to instruct or advise on individual financial decisions. Its purpose is to provide general understanding so readers can ask better questions, seek appropriate professional guidance, and make informed choices based on their unique circumstances.

Risk Disclosure

Homeownership and mortgage financing involve financial risk. While FHA loans are designed to increase access to homeownership and provide flexible qualification standards, they do not eliminate risk, and outcomes may vary based on individual circumstances, market conditions, and personal financial decisions. Purchasing or refinancing a home requires a long-term financial commitment and should be evaluated carefully.

Housing markets can fluctuate. Property values may increase or decrease over time, and there is no guarantee that a home will appreciate in value. Economic conditions, interest rate changes, local market factors, and unforeseen events can affect property values, mortgage payments, and resale opportunities. Borrowers should be prepared for the possibility that home values may remain flat or decline during certain periods.

Mortgage payments represent a fixed obligation that must be met regardless of changes in income, employment status, health, or personal circumstances. Failure to make mortgage payments may result in late fees, credit damage, default, or foreclosure. Borrowers should ensure they have adequate income stability, savings, and contingency planning before entering into any mortgage obligation.

FHA loans include mortgage insurance, which increases the total cost of borrowing. While mortgage insurance enables access to lower down payments and more flexible credit standards, it may remain in place for a significant portion of the loan term unless refinanced or otherwise removed under applicable guidelines. Borrowers should understand how mortgage insurance affects monthly payments and long-term costs.

Refinancing, selling, or leveraging home equity is not guaranteed to be available in the future. These options depend on market conditions, interest rates, credit profile, equity levels, and lender requirements at the time of action. Borrowers should not assume future refinancing opportunities or equity access when making initial homeownership decisions.

Rental income, including income from multi-unit properties or converted rentals, is not guaranteed. Vacancies, maintenance costs, market conditions, tenant behavior, and regulatory changes can impact rental cash flow. Borrowers considering rental strategies should evaluate these risks carefully and avoid relying on projected rental income for financial stability.

This book does not provide investment advice or predict financial outcomes. All examples and scenarios are illustrative only and should not be relied upon as forecasts or guarantees. Readers are responsible for conducting their own due diligence and seeking professional advice when appropriate.

By choosing to pursue homeownership or mortgage financing, readers acknowledge the presence of risk and accept responsibility for their financial decisions. The author and publisher are not responsible for any losses, damages, or adverse outcomes resulting from actions taken based on the information provided in this book.

This disclosure is intended to promote informed decision-making, not discourage homeownership. Understanding risk is a critical part of using FHA loans responsibly and sustainably.

www.ingramcontent.com/pod-product-compliance
Lightning Source LLC
La Vergne TN
LVHW022009200926
848481LV00007B/2298